811. How to dance in this
54   rarefied air
CRUSZ

Guelph Public Library

RIENZI CRUSZ has long been admired as one of the greatest poets to have emerged from Sri Lanka. Romantic yet also ironic, imbued with a unique brand of earthy humour, and an abiding sense of mortality and transience, his poetry pays homage to both the island home of his ancestors and his adopted country of Canada. Rendering the ordinary into the extraordinary, his poetic images linger on in memory, portraying the anguish of the displaced artist. Rienzi Crusz came to Canada in 1965. He was educated at the Universities of Ceylon, London, Toronto, and Waterloo, at the last of which he was the Reference Librarian. He is the author of twelve volumes of poetry. He lives in Waterloo.

BOOKS BY RIENZI CRUSZ

Flesh and Thorn

Elephant and Ice

Singing Against the Wind

A Time for Loving

Still Close to the Raven

The Rain Doesn't Know Me Any More

Beatitudes of Ice

Insurgent Rain : Selected Poems 1974-1996

Gambolling With the Divine

Lord of the Mountain: The Sardiel Poems

Enough to Be Mortal Now

Love Where the Nights Are Green

HOW TO DANCE IN THIS RAREFIED AIR

poems

Rienzi Crusz

Introduction by Linda Hutcheon

MAWENZI HOUSE

©2017 Rienzi Crusz

Introduction ©2017 Linda Hutcheon

Except for purposes of review, no part of this publication may be reproduced in any form without prior permission of the publisher.

We acknowledge the support of the Canada Council for the Arts for our publishing program. We also acknowledge support from the Government of Ontario through the Ontario Arts Council.

811.54 CRUSZ

Cover design by Michael Crusz

Library and Archives Canada Cataloguing in Publication

Crusz, Rienzi, 1925-, author

    How to dance in this rarefied air / Rienzi Crusz.

Poems.

Issued in print and electronic formats.

ISBN 978-1-988449-05-0 (softcover).--ISBN 978-1-988449-08-1 (HTML)

    I. Title.

PS8555.R87H69 2017   C811'.54   C2017-901857-4

                                                                         C2017-901858-2

Printed and bound in Canada by Coach House Printing

                    Mawenzi House Publishers Ltd.
                        39 Woburn Avenue (B)
                      Toronto, Ontario M5M 1K5
                                Canada
                      www.mawenzihouse.com

In memory
of my dear friend and mentor
Chelva Kanaganayakam

Words

    as slippery as smooth grapes
    words exploding in the light
    like dormant seeds waiting
    in the vaults of vocabulary,
    alive again, and giving life:
    once again the heart distills them.

PABLO NERUDA

Imagery, delivery, vocabulary spring from the body and the past of the writer and gradually become the very reflexes of his art. Thus under the name of style a self-sufficient language is evolved which has its roots only in the depths of the author's personal and secret mythology.

ROLAND BARTHES

How to Dance in this Rarefied Air is a collection setting out my poetics and modes of writing, my journey as a poet writing in Canada.

It offers a poetic that was fashioned to meet the demands of a poet in the cusp of two worlds. Hence, the songs of exile, idioms of defiance and survival, poems that attempt to cover the pain and promise of the immigrant encounter. Beyond meeting the basic demands of diaspora writing, I have also moved into other major themes with books on love (*Love Where the Nights Are Green*), politics (*Lord of the Mountain: The Sardiel Poems*), nature (*Don't Tell Me that I'm Not an Elephant*), religion (*Gambolling With the Divine*), poetics, and life (*Enough to Be Mortal Now*), elegies (*Coming Through the Shadows*). Overall, my poetic should reveal a poetic mythology of synthesis and accommodation of cultures, what it is to live "in this igloo of heaven" with the happy "idioms of the sun."

RIENZI CRUSZ

Contents

INTRODUCTION BY LINDA HUTCHEON
"Encounters" with Rienzi Crusz *xv*

I Am Now Balancing on Ice with a Poem in My Hand *1*
Obsession *3*
Ode to the Muse *5*
In a Weathervane Idiom *6*
Like a Hound Dog *8*
How to Dance in This Rarefied Air *9*
Elegy for the Poems That Got Away *12*
Carpe diem *14*
Where Adam First Touched the Finger of God *16*
Beyond Hyperbole Beyond Poetry *18*
After the K W Writer's Award #2 *19*
The Sun-Man's Poetic Five Ways *21*
The Nowhere Man *24*
For a Poet Friend Trashed by a Humbling Wind *26*
The Elephant Who Would Be a Poet *27*
Poetics for the Doubting One *28*
The Child Who Would Be a Poet *30*
Critique in Crystal *31*
Seven Ways of Looking at a Poet *32*
The Divine Equation *35*

There's Always a Water Bead in the Cactus   *38*

Apollo, the Mynah-Bird, Who Wanted to Be a Poet   *40*

"Rienzi, sometimes the master learns from the pupil—Love,
Mike"   *43*

The *Koha* Sings Only in Season   *45*

Only the Gesture, My Love   *47*

These Roses Are the Colour of Blood   *48*

Poetry Behind Bars   *49*

Four Eyes Looking at a Crow   *51*

If You Want the Flame to Dance Forever   *54*

Poem in the Light of Total Darkness   *55*

Roots   *57*

The Interview   *58*

The Opposite Men   *60*

Poem for the Faltering Man   *61*

The Creative Process   *62*

Going for Broke   *63*

A Contrary Silence   *64*

"Know your own bone"—Thoreau   *65*

Death of a Poet   *68*

Remains of an Asian Poet Writing in Canada   *70*

Elegy for the Unfinished Poem   *72*

Poetry Reading at Scarborough College   *73*

Requiem for the Passionate Ones   *75*

"Dark with excessive bright"   *77*

Legacy   *80*

Acknowledgements   *83*

INTRODUCTION
"Encounters" with Rienzi Crusz

Encounter is a key word, so to speak, that opens many doors into
Rienzi Crusz's rich poetic world. In that world, his Sun-Man and
Winter-Man are in constant encounter, for Sri Lanka and Canada
have formed this poet, just as surely as his Portuguese and Sinha-
lese parents in Sri Lanka formed the person. Rienzi Crusz was des-
tined to be a cultural hybrid even before his emigration to Canada.

My own memorable first encounter with Rienzi Crusz's world
was via his bracing poems—this very theme of hybrid identity and
immigration—a theme he approaches with what I have always
found to be an entrancing mixture of elegy and irony. For instance,
in a poem entitled "Conversations with God About My Pres-
ent Whereabouts," the elegiac and the ironic mingle with satiric
potency:

True, I often miss
the sensuous touch of fingers
on the shying touch-me-not,
the undergrowth's pink badge of bruise,
cacophony of crows,
the rain that pelted my thin bones.

But I am perfect now.
Seduced on shaven grass,
my barbecue glows
like a small hell,
the pork chops kindle,
the Molson cool,
I wear the turban of urban pride.

xv

In this new volume of poetry, *How to Dance in This Rarified Air,* the ironic and the elegiac are still strong, but even stronger is the commitment to encounter—but now encounter is meant more in the sense of refusing separate ways and accepting that he is *both* the past and the present, Sri Lanka and Canada. "Here on undivided ground, / we'll fashion our own mythologies," he writes—and so he has. Both cultures colour (brilliantly) and people (enchantingly) his poetic imagination: the ever-present elephants, coconut milk and mango share imaginative space with Canadian earmuffs, gloves, and snow boots. That said, with memory and time has come the even stronger realization of the blessed power of the poetic imagination to retrieve the distant and the past:

the fierce and aching poetry
of heart and mind and soul have trumped
this geography of exile   taken back
the extravagant sun

In this same poem we are offered intertwined metaphors from both worlds, here unabashedly presented in echoing competition with Shakespeare's own love sonnets:

If I should compare you
to the pyracantha in wedding dress,
its firethorn blaze,
spring lamb in giddy dance,
the backyard maple's summer face,
the August moon peeping through the apple tree,
cardinal on the wire fence in Santa Claus red,
sweet flesh of mango coconut milk . . .

This lush, image-rich passage is from one of the love poems to his wife, Anne, which happens to be one of the first of his poems I ever read. In the engaging film about him called *A Work in Progress,* he

xvi

jokes that his wife complained that he wrote poems to or about everyone but her. The one he wrote for her—"Legacy: for Anne"—is also the one that the Serbian Canadian composer Ana Sokolovic has now set to music as part of her song cycle of Canadian poetry entitled "dawn always begins in the bones." Fittingly, this very same poem is reprinted here and ends this book, as yet another lasting part of Rienzi Crusz's poetic legacy.

Anne and other family members feature in these new poems, as in so many others before them, keeping him grounded, giving him perspective, anchoring him in the physical, corporeal world where "truth" is "in the uncompromising gesture" and a warm hug "trumps the fire of words," even for a poet. It is to these loved ones that he tries to explain why he writes, why there can be no such thing as exaggeration in poetry, for poetry is where one can "savour the mad beautiful dance of metaphor, / imaginative leaps." His family, his friends, his students, and his fellow poets are all part of his poetic world. So too is his deep Catholic faith. All are encountered by us, through these poems.

But it is as a poet and as a lover of poetry that we most vividly encounter Rienzi Crusz in this new book. This is a man who said of the first poem he ever wrote (in 1967), called "The Unhappy Cataloguer," composed while working as a library assistant at the University of Toronto: "At the time I didn't even realize it was a poem." We all know now that it most certainly was. The fact that this volume is dedicated to the memory of the late Chelva Kanaganayakam, my colleague and his fellow Sri Lankan and friend, is movingly appropriate. These poems speak to Rienzi Crusz's identity as a poet—both Sri Lankan and Canadian—a poet whose work Kanaganayakam admired, enjoyed, studied, and taught to generations of students at the University of Toronto. His fine 1997 book, *Dark Antonyms and Paradise: The Poetry of Rienzi Crusz*, brings together his reading of the personal, political, and poetic to illuminate the work of the poet he considered one of the most important of diasporic writers.

xvii

This new volume is one that Kanaganayakam would have appreciated immensely—and found in it confirmation for his interpretation of the poet's aesthetic. *How to Dance in This Rarefied Air*, as the author's note openly states, aims to set out his "poetics and modes of writing," his "journey as a poet writing in Canada" but actually writing "in the cusp of two worlds." So, the Rienzi Crusz I first encountered is here fully revealed in what he calls his "poetic mythology of synthesis and accommodation of cultures, what it is to live 'in this igloo of heaven' with the happy 'idioms of the sun.'" But this is also a collection of poems that self-reflexively addresses the themes of creativity, memory, and time—in short, poems that many would see as illustrating the poet's "late style." At the age of 91, he is perhaps allowed such a designation, and he chooses here to write a poem called "Carpe diem." It is true that death—that of his father, his friends, and, in time, his own—haunts the volume. But poetry and life together dominate.

Many of this poet's past works have been personal, and this collection is no different. The journey begins with a poem about his birth and the good omens promising strong "creative juices." But what is amusingly called his "first poem"—consisting of his "furious cheering" at the midwife's ministrations—is witnessed by a silent, pensive father. In yet another poem, the poet is presented as "the one born screaming / with a poem in his throat," who "learnt the rhythm of words" from fables read by his mother, and who

keeps faith in the dance of words
through his summer years,
    and when life's autumn comes
and winter blows,

writes the poem
    he has become.

xviii

The mortal poet becomes the immortal poem; its language, its imagery are what will remain of the poet. As the book's epigraph, from Roland Barthes, puts it: "under the name of style a self-sufficient language is evolved which has its roots only in the depths of the author's personal and secret mythology." As this suggests, these poems are deeply autobiographical and personal but mostly in the sense that they are about the writer and his writing life. For instance, there is a poem about his advice to high school students wanting to be poets. There are his inspired poems about seeking inspiration. There is a song of generous and heart-felt praise for the artists who inspire him, whose words seduce him away from family and nature and society, in one poem, and, in another, teach him "how to dance in this rarefied air"—that is, with passion, silence, blood, and song. He rejects the admired T S Eliot and his wasteland modernism: "your ransom will not be paid," he boldly tells him. Instead, he will read and enjoy and be inspired by the likes of Shakespeare, Milton, the psalms, Montes de Oca, Pablo Neruda, Rabindranath Tagore, Dylan Thomas, Gerard Manley Hopkins, Federico Garcia Lorca, Rainer Maria Rilke, Cesar Vallejo, Michael Ondaatje, and Derek Walcott.

His favoured dwelling may be a "word house," but it is no less real for that: in it, he would write his muse's name in the style of graffiti—"the heart raw and public." Words have power and materiality for this poet:

We embrace words
as we would weapons,
a pin, a shotgun, a machete
for each fighting day.
Until we have words
without fear or favour,
weathervane meanings,

we'll continue to tremble
in our uncivilized arguments of living,
our known condition of death.

In this powerfully verbal world, he asks, does the word hunt the
poet or does the poet hunt the word? He answers, in "Elegy for
the Poems That Got Away"—with its memorable metaphors and
truths—that we "write our lives in prose" while the Muse laughs
at "images exploding in my face, / bird song smothered in the egg."
At 91, the poet contemplates age and what he so strikingly calls
"the body's slow disarmament"—and he encounters and faces both
with courage and compassion. In the end, it is the spirit of creation
and imagination that continues keeping him alive. In "Poem for
the Faltering Man" he writes:

I'm balancing
on the brink

death and panorama
around and below.

But faltering legs
dangerous landscape

or final decisions
will not make the poem.

Only the supreme electricity
of doubt,

those screaming moments
when wind, muscle and mind

xx

argue
whether to keep me up there

alive.

Doubt, imagination, engagement combine to do precisely that, with humility, grace and confidence in the power of love and poetry—when, once again, as in "Poem in the Light of Total Darkness," the poem takes over the poet:

As for my absence,
the voluntary stones in my mouth,
I know the prison of sunlight,
so I let the night
that holds the green poem
like a woman in its arms,
speak with love, with pure eloquence.

But those early themes of hybrid identity persist, and with age and impending end, they do so with no less of the elegiac and the ironic, but certainly with more acceptance, even resolution of duality:

I hear the immigrant's voice, sweet and clear
as bamboo reed,
the elephant's trumpet
shattering the dark silences
of the snow lands
—not without doubt, without human regret:
"And so, you who never listened
to my green song,
behold the dream:

xxi

me, strangled by my own words
under a brown comforter,
the paramedics carrying
the mangled poem of my body,

and you sitting up
and listening at last."

Here the poet—who now "knows the colour of death"—faces the end of his creative life, if not the end of his poetry (which will live on). But the words of Pablo Neruda, which form the other epigraph to this volume, echo right to the end:

words exploding in the light
like dormant seeds waiting
in the vaults of vocabulary,
alive again, and giving life

This book's moving encounter with Rienzi-Crusz-the-poet marks the planting of many a word seed "alive again, and giving life."

LINDA HUTCHEON,
University Professor Emeritus of English
and Comparative Literature
University of Toronto

xxii

I Am Now Balancing on Ice with a Poem in My Hand

For Dad

All agreed
that the omens at my birth were good:
the cow calved within minutes
of my arrival, the caretaker spoke of udders
hanging from a full moon.
The old gardener cried sadhu to the sun
for turning his roses redder than blood,
though he couldn't understand
why their thorns were longer
and sharper this year.
The maid giggled into the verandah
with six warm eggs cupped in her hands,
first offerings
of the black Leghorn pullets.

The family astrologer scaled me in Libra,
promised creative juices
strong as the current of the Mahaveli.
My mother remarked
that I seemed to have danced in her womb,
and the fat midwife froze
when she slapped my buttocks
and heard my furious cheering
for her expert manipulations.

Only my father was silent,
holding the joy and the torment of the omens

in his eyes,
and, having witnessed the first poem,
silently wondered
when and where, if ever,
I would fashion my others.

Obsession

When there's laughter and banter
around the kitchen table   sunshine
hugging the old maple   gazebo with waiting arms,
the tricycle child, my neighbour, old McIver,
walking happily in his khaki shorts and spent bones;

when I love the parka of the sun,
the forsythia's saffron face,
how the butterfly tree
seduces the loafing monarchs
the magic of popsicle disappearing
on Maria's drooling tongue,

why return
to the comfort of the womb?
My den's embracing silence solitude
with only
those great exponents of the word,
poets of thought and rhythm,
where Dali's *Crucifixion* looks down on me
like a blessing   a lone fly on the wall
holds its silence, and my dog, Roshan,
sleeps at my feet
in spread-eagled splendour;

why do I again and again
escape my wife, my kids summer's warm largesse,
and fall to this seduction?
What dramatic lines, scenarios

3

are you throwing at me, good Bard of Avon?
And Walcott, my friend, why do you snare me
with your soulful words so touched
by your Caribbean sun?

Pablo, compatriot of sun and rain, the good earth,
please, please, stop seducing me
with your magic metaphors,
odes to your stinking socks, artichoke and onion
on your kitchen table;
and my Sri Lankan brother, Michael O,
keep silent. I love your narratives,
your clinical way with words.
Your great poem: The cinnamon peeler's wife.

Ode to the Muse

If I should write your name
only in graffiti, I would write
with much love. I'm talking
of spontaneous combustion, the kind
of explosion arranged by the gods,
the poem a Roman candle.

In this word house, the shining parlour
with its ancient chandelier, Kashmir carpet,
sings no more sweetly
than the flushing toilet, the garbage
grumbling in the can. Together,
a mighty symphony seeps through these cabook walls.

Give me the sunflower mad in the sun,
give me also a patch of shadow
to cool my burning feet;
if there be pain, let me hear its melody,
if imperfection boasts, a streak of lightning
to tell me of sudden ends.

So let me write your name
in graffiti, a style
with no beginning, no end,
ribs pried apart
the heart raw and public.

5

In a Weathervane Idiom

You talk of fire
I say arson;
you call it love,
I read lust;
you call it sex,
I hear rape;
you call it neatness
(and say it's next to godliness)
I suspect mediocrity;
you describe laughter,
I learn the sign of madness;
you call it wisdom.
I see a fool.

Listen to the word
in the soft green womb of the valley,
now shout it
in the rarefied air of the mountain top;
listen to the silence
outside the curved belly
of the woman heavy with child,
now pin your ears to her belly button
and hear the pounding of a new heartbeat,
the hissing waterfall of baby blood.

We embrace words
as we would weapons,
a pin, a shotgun, a machete

for each fighting day.
Until we have words
without fear or favour,
weathervane meanings,
we'll continue to tremble
in our uncivilized arguments of living,
our known condition of death.

Like a Hound Dog

The word
hunts the poet—
dark alleys
smokey pubs
blonde corn fields
rice paddies sizzling in the sun,
wherever;

conjures
a cemetery
of dead autumn leaves
or his front-yard catalpa undressing
to winter's fierce gaze
or his pet dog, Sparky, leaping
from its ashes
on the fireplace mantel,
whatever;

or the poet, the word?

in either case
there is a killing
and a resurrection
like the golden Digger wasp
that paralyzes the spider,
lays a single egg
in its belly
and waits patiently
for its waspy poem.

How to Dance in This Rarefied Air

How he jabs his thick forefinger
   into my poetic
as if it were a breastbone.
   O God, how it hurts;

cups his eyes
   against my passionate burning,
the bougainvillea's profusion,
   elephant
as a rogue in heat.

My words, it would seem,
   elude him by a generation;
I would walk only
   in shaded byways or exotic arbours,
the poem jaundiced
   without the blood of a new idiom.

What he wants
   is wasteland:
white, scrubbed, frontier;
whose poems
   must deconstruct to bare bone,
the flesh and blood laid out separately
   to dry like fish
in the noonday sun.

No. I will not desert
   those wintered killing fields,

the spilled blood sweeter
   among the paddies, the frangipani,
upside-down elephant
   squinting at the sun.
Noble Eliot, you might as well
   rest in peace,
your ransom will not be paid.

My ear to the ground
   and I hear the drumbeat of Avon,
mad Hamlet strut and nurse
   his eloquent pain;
Milton, hammering Lucifer
   to a perfect poetic, a perfect Hell.

Wounded, give me the psalms of David,
   words to learn by rote, comfort the dark sargassum
of my days,
   how the valley of death
passes like a bad dream.

I am still here, Montes de Oca,
   my beautiful wild Mexican bard,
belting my boisterous song;
   and Pablo, hug me again,
show me the true metaphors
   of sun and rain,
how to throw my bread on the waters,
   circle the world with a poem.

Speak to me, Rabindranath,
   I need to hear your distant voice,

bask under your stunning skies;
and Kahlil, I haven't forgotten
your wisdom that must laugh
and weep, bow one's head to a child.

And Dylan, do I ever love the melody
of your song, your riotous book of words;
good Manley, sing, sing, sing,
I'm all ears and silent;
Lorca, my friend,
tell me the secrets of "Duende",
ask the spirit to stab my words again.

Rilke, take me gently
into the depths of myself,
the soundless paths,
how to listen, listen, listen;
as for you, Vallejo,
teach me the thunder of silence,
the value of the spilled blood,
how to dance in this rarefied air.

Elegy for the Poems That Got Away

Somewhere in that twilight
between sleep and awakening,
or walking with the sun
between my legs, head in the clouds,
they come like lightning
and darkly vanish—
for the Muse to hold her ribs in laughter
at images exploding in my face,
bird song smothered in the egg.

Some come alone,
one lean lily in the field,
or red in clusters,
or shapes like bullfrog heads,
buttock line perfect
under Naomi's baby doll silk;

or in the confusion of fire,
water lapping stone,
hurricane in the cumulus cloud,
the earth rooting corn
in its moist belly;

metaphors from pink daylight,
a dog loose in high noon,
raven in the evening,
night shaping saucer eyes for the owl;

or they come with the smell

jasmine, raw wood,
or Charlie behind her ears,
sometimes the barnyard signature,
cow dung at the foot of the rose;

out of the house
full of icons, the mysterious sound,
the ghetto
spilling gut syllables,
nuances from marble in moonlight,
the profound word
whispered in the hut.

Gone before they come,
broken before they are made,
we cannot hold the lightning
of the gods,
a mercury too quick
for our clumsy hands,
and so mourn the deaths of butterflies
in chrysalis,

and write our lives in prose,
the stone in our palm
still the hard mineral thing,
the dream   grounded
like a broken bird,
and we sleep
as somewhere in the Trinidadian wood
a poem sings
under the trembling wings
of the hummingbird.

Carpe diem

I pass yesterday's crooked milepost,
    take in night for erasure,
fireflies, timeless hour
    of dreams.
Where closure marks
    the death of pain,
and sweetness lingers on.

And tomorrow?
    Will monsoon rain
havoc among the tender paddies,
    expectations
slip like jello
        through my grasping fingers?

Time   tomorrow,
    you are the mercury hour,
and I'll not try
    to read your tarot soul or clasp
your ghostly hands.

So, today
        is the hugging moment,
when dawn walks in
    like a dear friend coming up the driveway;
today is the apple
    between my teeth, song
fevered in my throat, the baila
    that moves my old legs
to muscular dance.

And when the good earth
    sizzles in its high-noon fire,
I shall laze under this old Maple,
    read Neruda, and think
of Haputale's gentle rain, embracing mist,
    how poetry stalks the elephant,
fashions the raven into profound metaphor.

and then at evening,
    I'll still forget
the clocking hour, hunt memory
    for the small boy chasing the sand crabs
with blue ocean
    roaring in his ears,

honey in the fruit bat's mouth,
    dusk that takes in the raven
to autograph a Gauguin sky,

and remember
    the sun, the song, the dance,
the dance, the song, the sun.

Where Adam First Touched the Finger of God

Junction. The road forks
like a wishbone:
I choose neither, refuse
the destinies in separate highways.
And so I go for a space
In no-man's land,
the immediate centre that seems to belong
to no man, and every man.
Here the division ends,
journey's anonymous oasis
where Adam shall continue
his fallen history.

Where the robin shall sing
with the voice of the paddy-bird,
the oak wear the fruit of jak,
the crow soar with the eagle;
where the dreaming minds shall have a choice
of coloured snows,
children play with old men,
and the sophisticated young
will again learn their wisdom
from infants, their sanity
from grandfather fables.

I will not travel again
the separate paths of the sun,
the cruel geography of East and West

that blurs the mountain's blue mist,
the green of lush valleys below.
Does it matter which way
the road turns?
There will always be another Grail,
another song, another weeping.
Wherever, the wind will never let go
its secrets. Here on undivided ground,
we'll fashion our own mythologies.

Beyond Hyperbole Beyond Poetry

For Anne

If I should compare you
to the pyracantha in wedding dress,
its firethorn blaze,
spring lamb in giddy dance,
the backyard maple's summer face,
the August moon peeping through the apple tree,
cardinal on the wire fence in Santa Claus red,
sweet flesh of mango coconut milk,

do not speak to me of hyperbole,
exotic metaphor, empty words—
consider only the language of poets
when fevered in the embrace
of an enduring love:

those caring words always spilling
from your lexicon of love,
mannerisms of patient grace,
your giving, your smiles in dissent,
your long kitchen hours,
your silent moments for the Divine,

your soul

beyond hyperbole,
beyond poetry.

After the K W Writer's Award #2

This piece of sun,
this shimmering bronze statue,
K W Writer's Award—
Sculptor Denny at his best,
the Mayor nodding his bald head
and saying: "Yes, yes, let him have his moment,
let this be Kitchener's finest literary hour
at the Rotunda.
Flag the hall, let in the enthusiastic guests,
stoke them
with donuts and Colombian coffee."

I bring the trophy home.
My son instantly shapes the statue's breasts
to Jaffna mangoes,
questions its exaggerated buttocks;
there's a no-big-deal smile
on my wife's face
as she strongly suggests
the practical use of the trophy's weight
for breaking coconuts.

What now
for my happiness, my pride?
Why do I hear Milton
whispering into my ear:
"the last great infirmity
of the noble mind"—

So be it.
And why Rilke are you laughing, forgiving,
arguing against all victory?

I recall my next-door neighbour saying
that his one ambition
was to own a double-garage home—
He has it now,
but is plagued with a new desire:
a cottage in Georgian Bay.

When will happiness finally tame
the elusive demons of desire?
So, don't ask me
if I am happy—
tomorrow, happiness will be left behind
like some beautiful child abandoned,
as I burn the midnight oil,
chasing after the Governor General's Award.

The Sun-Man's Poetic Five Ways

1

Who, when darkness fell thick over the dead,
stole into the city cemetery
to read the tombstones by pencil light,
hoping to find the heart of a poem.
Nothing. Until something ghoulish screamed,
cracking the pogonip air, ricochetting
from headstone to headstone,
and the shaking man fumbled for his nest of bones,
pinched his cold thighs
to discover his own blood-beat.

He wrote in his notebook:
"The dead are safe as the sleeping soil.
The poem is in the scream
that make the living pinch their thighs."

2

Who, brown and strolling
down a Toronto street,
came up against these black vinyl jackets
with mouths hurling their *PAKI PAKI* words like knives;
colour of offenders' eyes: hazel, blue, blue.
Hair: all long, like Jesus, down the nape;
estimated educational background: TV's *Police Story*
starring Angie Dickinson;
home address: Paradise Blvd, Toronto.
Possible motives: kicks.

"So much poetry in the trajectory of crow sounds."

3

Who, visiting the Dehiwela Zoo in Colombo,
came across the long twin cage for carnivora
where jungle peace hung like a thread
on a small connecting door;
which, in the interests of poetry
he stealthily unlatched:
and the hot paws swung like hammers,
the tiger's jugular first to spring a leak,
the lion blotting the blood of victory
on his thick mane,
then quietly lying down
to arrange his own death like a king.

And he wrote in his notebook:
"So much poetry in a small sliding door."

4

Who, standing back,
watched the raw hunks of meat
fly from the zoo keeper's hands,
the panther already nosing for marrow
under the black goat skin.
Old ladies, children, lovers,
tighten their knot
as they move closer
to take in the evening's ritual.
Then the first escaping cry, the roar
outside bars,

the knot suddenly untangling
bodies running without direction.

And he wrote in his notebook:
"The door again. So much poetry in doors."

5

Who broke journey late one night
at this wayside tea boutique in Sri Lanka,
hears the host stammer in whispers:
"It is out tonight."
Unheeding, continued journey
when the road suddenly narrowed
to a mere jungle path,
and hundred yards away
breathed this massive grey obstruction
with blood clotting in his eyes,
trunk hurled up
in the killing ways of the rogue elephant.
Up a tree,
the man jotted in his notebook:

'The poem happens
when the hulking door closes,
and the poet writes his poem
in the high architecture of trees."

The Nowhere Man

I am not there
to listen to the blue music
of your Indian Sea,
the rumble the hoot of elephant
by the shores of the *Heen Weva*,

But I am there.

I am not there
to hear the rowdy language of the crow,
the earthy wisdom
of the drunken lavatory coolies
discussing politics
at the back of a crowded bus.

But I am there.

I am not there
to taste the sweet mango
or drink the healing milk
of the king coconut,
savour your exotic rice and curry,
your buffalo curd and palmyrah honey.

But I am there.

True. I am here
with my head under a raining snow.
True. I have earmuffs, snow boots, gloves,
snow mask to keep out

the blistering snow from my black eyes.
But I am still cold
and I am not here.

I am there.

I am no longer the nowhere man,
for the fierce and aching poetry
of heart and mind and soul have trumped
this geography of exile   taken back
the extravagant sun.

For a Poet Friend Trashed by a Humbling Wind

After reading your poem enclosed
in your letter of September 4, 2006,
I sketched Golgotha
on its white margins—
and the humbling wind came again,
but the hanging tree refused
to give up its hero.

Once again,
lightning knifed the earth,
made fire in the chalice of the lily,
scythed Roman knees in shame,
but the naked man hung still,
the triumph of nailed body to wood.

My friend, listen
to the hard poem in pain:
the stone sings in its solid prison,
the bog, shifting sands,
carry their deaths
in small murmurs of song.

If you have no altar,
make one, the harder the better.
Pain is like the hanging tree,
a vantage point that looks at darkness,
conjures the Golgotha Man
trembling in his triumph,
bruised hardness
that is first to know, feel,
see the resurrection.

The Elephant Who Would Be a Poet

High noon. The piranha sun
cuts to the bone.
Anula, the heaving elephant
froths from the mouth.
The logging ends.

Without a command
he eases his huge body to the ground,
rolls over,
and makes new architecture
with his thick legs,
four columns vertical
to the sun.

The confused mahout
refuses the poem in this new equilibrium
this crazy theatre of the mind,

this new way
of looking at the world,
upside down.

Poetics for the Doubting One

Yes—mine are stories
to storm your walnut eyes,
make light your serious head.

How away from the mauling sun
I squat under a *murunga* tree
and wait—for Puspa, my favourite mother elephant,
to come along and discuss family affairs,
hers and mine;

wait for Shakunta, the mammoth tusker,
to lay me down gently
and extract my painful wisdom tooth.
Refuse your invading thoughts:
my mental gibberish, the sun's suffusing madness?

OK. So I also dismiss prophecies:
your two magpies suddenly darting from nowhere
and alighting on my left shoulder;
no ears either
to your cats wailing on the parapet wall,
or the raven's raucous cry from the jambu tree.
Granted,
my beloved father died under similar omens.

Why do I laugh
seeing you walk barefooted
in a white sari to the Temple
to listen to the old monk

recite his *seth kavi*
for your father's return to his family?

Why refuse the magic
of your housewarming rituals,
the clay pot of milk boiling over
to sign the kitchen floor?

Woman, if you can walk with the superstitious stars
bound to your shapely ankles,
let the intransigent moon
havoc in your storm of curls,
birds speak in tongues
of hollow oracles,
why can't you for once say yes
to the god of imagination,
madness that can pirouette on a pinhead
and believe:
an elephant that's a superb psychiatrist,
another that thinks
he's a professional dentist?

Listen. At the margins of poetry
are lies, modes of ridicule,
foul words, sweet nothings;
but savour the mad beautiful dance of metaphor,
imaginative leaps, primeval chaos—
for at the centre
lies truth
still and uncompromising as desert stone.

The Child Who Would Be a Poet

For Michael

High expectation—
  his mother praying
that at last her son would cross
  that first threshold of civilization,
sit on his brand new potty
  and quietly shit away his pablum.

High expectation—
  his father's fervent hope
that his son would gently go
  with his mother's exhortations,
discipline his bowel movements
  and reduce the pamper bill
to zero.

Secretly
  (without an applause muscle moving)
the old poet exults
  as his son quickly arranges
the shining white bowl on his head
  and parades the room duly hatted.

Both father and mother
  now seemed to understand
the true nature
  of art, childhood and violence,
as a new and disturbing poem
  havocks in mother's incredulous eyes.

Critique in Crystal

"I've read your book *Elephant and Ice*
with much interest," says the redhead co-ed
to the Sun-Man poet. "I've also seen
your most recent poem, 'The Elephant
Who Would Be a Poet'—
The elephant image seems to rampage
throughout your work."

"Here's a little something for you,"
handing over a small box
wrapped in sea-green paper
with Santa Claus romping all over it.
The silk bow was close
to Indian Ocean blue.
"Thank you," says the poet graciously,
unwrapping the gift quickly
to discover a tiny crystal elephant
basking in the translucent light
of its own body.

Pressing, the poet asks;
"What do you think of my poetry?"
"Look again at the elephant
as it stands on your desk."
He did.

A very lopsided beast
was staring back at him with curious eyes.

Seven Ways of Looking at a Poet

1
Yes. He is the same man
   you saw last morning at the Coffee Shoppe
in the company of a doughnut, hot coffee and a cigarette,
   but one you do not see at night
sipping cold coffee and hunting for words
   to sing of the cobwebbed symmetry of stars,
loafing fireflies, babies
   bawling in their mother's arms,
of gun smoke, raven and elephant,
   curve of buttock, lovers
under a blue moon, refugees
   dying in the Darfur sun.

2
Demosthenes
   with stones in his mouth
who turns his stammering beginnings,
   his boisterous duel with bugger words,
intrusive images those
   with barefaced lies in their bones,
to the magic
   of profound words, resounding rhetoric.

3
Who sees the world
   a blob, a blur,
then clearly in daylight

as he discovers its heartbeat
on the kitchen table—
    the upside-down bottle of ketchup,
water glasses, pepper and salt,
    bowl of apples
waiting for their juicy deaths.

4
How he crosses a frontier
    in search of a new Jerusalem,
matches his tumultuous soul
    against howling winds, raging cold,
a thick shroud of snow,
    to grasp his immigrant dream
without ever forgetting
    the small cabook house
where he was born—
    the flame of bougainvillea
on his thick yard fence,
his kingdom of raven and elephant.

5
He's the one
    who first imagined God
as only in the solitude of the cloister,
    under the capuchin's soutane,
somewhere in the swirling incense
    of the cathedral's high altar,
then finds him
    amidst a rollicking crowd
in the village fair,

in the face of a grandpa standing by
a Ferris wheel of laughing children.

6

Who discovers
    the emptiness of words,
the ugly face of fakery
    in his narrative of the fisherman of Sri Lanka
shaped from photographs,
    his dictionary of words, jaded facts
from the computer's cold mouth
    after he meets an old man
sitting on a boulder in Mt Lavinia's beach,
    with salt in his fisherman's veins,
and a mouthful of fables
    about the catamaran men of the Indian sea.

7

Yes. He's the one born screaming
    with a poem in his throat,
who learnt the rhythm of words
    from Mother Goose fables
on his mother's knee,
    keeps faith in the dance of words
through his summer years,
    and when llife's autumn comes
and winter blows,

writes the poem
    he has become.

The Divine Equation

And towards the end,
between spasms
of asthmatic breath,
my father would talk

of God's fingerprints,
the "Divine Smudge,"
the jiggery of human kindness,
Zaccheus of the sycamore tree,

and mathematically,
of the "Divine Equation";

so, if you love
the perfume of the rose,
Its summer dalliance,
don't forget
its stem of thorns;

hug the cripple on the street,
never mind
his stump of legs, gnarled hands,
his empty tin cup,

only see God's exact sun
In his crooked shadow,
how his squiggly lines burgeon
to pure architecture;

see redemption
for the killing world,
and wait patiently
for the thunder to resolve
Into a sweet summer rain;

be happy
in solitude, if solitude is your way,
But keep your small ears open
to the vault of blue sky

and you'll hear
the clink and clash of rolling glass,
God playing marbles
with Moses and Aaron;

choose to pass
the lush green valleys
for the high nightmare mountain,
And there, slay your demons
of flesh and fear;

be the one
who'll, perhaps, write the embracing poem;
show them what happens
on Monkey Mountain,

how painted icons
melt like Icarus's wings
to the muted colours
of faith and love;

who'll fashion the raven's caw
to canary sweetness,
make the elephant walk
this Toronto boulevard in *Perehara* style.

There's Always a Water Bead in the Cactus

For my favourite students at College Avenue Secondary School, Woodstock

Daily,
come sun or rain,
snow or sleet,
Muse under your legs or nowhere,
you write, write for two hours.
So instructed the old poet.

Keep squeezing   squeezing
till something spills—
The stone will eventually give, perspire,
there's always a water-bead
in the cactus.

Relax. Let your muscles,
your mind
take off like a butterfly.
Patience, even if
you must pick your nose,
there's always a nugget
in the gumbo of words.

If the poem is shaping
to zero,
if the doodles, lines
are without geometry,
words without arms, legs or eyes,
if you cannot find
the heart of the poem

and everything looks
like the weather report: heavy cloud,
cold, windy,
precipitation 85%,

then tomorrow

tomorrow   the poem
tomorrow   the truth.

Apollo, the Mynah-Bird, Who Wanted to Be a Poet

All's well with Apollo,
except for his limited vocabulary.
He distrusts
   "LOVE" in word or deed,
refuses
   to echo the loving sound
in his throat.
   But swear, and he'll embrace the word
like an impatient lover.

The sun room's summer light,
   gourmet dinners
of live worms, golden millet,
   dead moths
harvested from under the porch light,
   have fashioned a patch
of Sri Lankan sun,
   a native backyard
in his brass-wire cage.

I say "LOVE"
   (trying the benefits of teaching
and learning by rote)
   but Apollo immediately falls
into a midnight silence;

I say "LOVE,"
   over and over again
like some Buddhist *Seth Kavi*,

but he would shake the sheen
of his black regal head, circle
   the room with his beady eyes
as if under siege.

"DAMN," I swear
   (thinking of all those other dumb birds
in my life)
   and Apollo squawks;
"DAMN,"
   He now cries "DAMN,"
whenever I enter or leave his presence.
   Trying some reverse psychology,
I slowly and softly say "DAMN,"

offering him some live worms
   to ease his adamant mind—
But he shouts back: "DAMN GOOD,"
   with an air of poetic impertinence.

I try the good word again.
   look deep into his urgent eyes
and say: "LOVE"—
   Quickly, as if from over the hedge
from our drunken neighbour's foul mouth comes "FUCK!"
"Nothing Futs," I swear,
   to which the bird immediately replies:
"DAMN GOOD!"

Last act.
   Venue: the sun room,
into which I invite a dear friend

for beer, pizza, and discussion.
But Apollo resents the intrusion,
    squawks incoherently, then settles down,
bows his thin head and shouts:
    Hello, Hello, "DAMN FOOL!"

I've not given up
    on the bird,
still wondering
    about his potential for beat poetry;
my cat, Pompei, however,
    has a dire alternative:
his old day dream
    of black strewn feathers, splintered beak
and mauled yellow feet.

"Rienzi, sometimes the master learns from the pupil— Love, Mike"

For Michael Estok

What have you learnt from me,
professor, mon ami?
The poet on the cover of your book
Poses with the abandon
of a banyan,
you looking like a young Keats
drinking in the sun.

I read your poems:
"Chansons Acadiennes,"
"Spells and Curses,"
the "Desperate Solidarities,"—
all lean and muscled like stallions, nowhere
near my fat sun, my hefty words,
my wounds red as immortelle.

So, what have you learnt, Sir?
You who sing nothing but the polished stone,
the exact chirrup of a dying cricket,
the subtle magic on the prairie's face
and always the kernel, the kernel,
husk and shell out on the rubbish heap.
All this genius, yours not mine.

I broke all the rules—
The sun chattering in my teeth,

my hair on fire,
the smell of elephant,
body and brain listening all the while
to the mad and searing order of words.

When I coloured, I coloured wildly,
feather of Ibis, the sun
with blood on its face.
When I killed, I mauled them to sleep,
could never shoot clean between the eyes.
The extravagant metaphor always mine,
mine like honey in the mouth.

The Koha Sings Only in Season

For Abdul Lodhi

Those long silences—
time when darkness closed
the windows of earth,
the nightly spangle of stars
and the mind stopped wondering, searching
for the truth behind
our cobwebbed lives, the joys
of our sunlight days;

when night's dark distemper
shadowed the *jambu* tree in the backyard
and turned its vermilion fruit
to nothing but a spray of obsidian eyes;
how the paddies once golden in the sun
now swayed in their thin charcoal bones;

when the river that laughed
and chased after with lusty arms
the open sea
could no longer hide
its now wrinkled face from the raven
and shared its karma with a lone elephant dead
by the waterless edge;

when the words would not come,
my metaphors flounder
and my thoughts look like naked mannequins;

when the poem would not write, the song
would not sing,
when my friend Abdul Lodhi
lost his life too soon, too soon
and I wasn't ready to write his elegy.

The *koha* sings only in season.

Cuckoo bird of morning song
trumpeter
to the Singhala New Year
you leave the night
to the guttural throat of the *Bakamoona*;

gone the memories
of the surgeon's knife,
morphine's dull bandage of pain;
it's the morning of a new day,
and I'll light the candles again, one by one,
pitch my canticles to high heaven,
and hitch my new words
to the rhythms of the Kandyan drums, the *baila* song.

Abdul Lodhi, I am writing your elegy at last.

Bakamoona: Sri Lankan fish owl
baila: type of music and dance first introduced by the Portugese to Sri lanka

Only the Gesture, My Love

For Anne

Love, if you wish to say to me:
"I love you darling"
Don't!
Just hug me
and let our bodies
explode your words
in utter silence.

What would you rather have?

Words
with the heart of the chameleon,
parables with no clear answers,
narratives that often dance
on the cusp of truth and falsehood,
the sometimes guttural noise of their stories

or

truth
in the uncompromising gesture:
a dimpled smile,
an old man's scowl,
a clenched fist,
a grandma with open arms,
a child's sneaky hands in the cookie jar,
a hug
that trumps the fire of words?

These Roses Are the Colour of Blood

She opened a vein
and planted a rose,

the thorns she kept
for herself.

In the embrace of the wound,
from bruising and bleeding,

poet and muse
make poetry.

Poetry Behind Bars

The big cats behind bars

Stand back,
watch the kingdoms in their smoking eyes,
limbs, how they move liquid
against the cage's cold ribs,
the dream
still hot in their chained muscles.

How Gemunu, the Bengal tiger,
crouches, as before the final leap
and even now in sleep
turns these grey bars
to tall blonde grass;

Kutti, the black panther,
shuts out the white moon
with its charcoal skin
as he sets fire to a wild pig
with diamond-torch eyes;

and Sheba, the old lioness,
takes back the Serengeti plains
from limb to zebra limb
with a single bellowing roar.

These are all ghosts, ghosts
of poems, imperial, revisited.
If you want the substantive thing,

the primeval dance of fire
let the animals out,
one by one.

Then will you gather
no blur of words,
deconstruction's frail white bones,
only raw feelings meanings
leaping with life and death,

art
which is "to do the dangerous thing."

Four Eyes Looking at a Crow

Blue eyes:
icicles on a naked branch
of the old maple;
a lone robin   forlorn
under an absent sun;
the snow geese squawking their way out
of the winter land.

Your closet
now home to parka, earmuffs, gloves,
snow boots impatient for new journeys
in the snow;
where the wintered slopes await
in cold silence
for supple limbs and skidding skis.

What do you think of the crow?

Black happening. Black happening:
the ugly walloping of wings in the thin air;
shadow bird
so contrary to sun and snow,
my cold pale skin;
prophet
of the black and broken moment,
the dumpster's grand metaphor,
how your raucous cawing, cawing, cawing
screams through my cold nerves.

Black eyes:
the king-coconut tree
heavy with the nectar of the gods;
where three magpies crowd the *jambu* tree
and twitter about wedding bells,
the embracing arms of the sun;
how the legend and love of the elephant
hovers like a blessing
over the sun land.

Your closet
home to cricket bats, tennis shoes,
faded sarongs, Bermuda shorts,
those other artifacts necessary to comb
the golden beaches of your Indian sea.

What do *you* think of the crow?

Gauguin magic: black wings
against a twilight sky;
bird of the sun   so close
to the seal-skin colour of my face;
squawking prophet of doom:

the scattered brood of chickens, one
in the gnarled embrace of the hawk;
those nightmares of thunder and lightning
announcing the coming storm.
Passionate bird, I hear the chorus of your lament
for a fallen one of your tribe;
true environmentalist, I salute you,
the way you dispose of our kitchen waste,

the road-side kills festering under an unforgiving sun.

and tell me
who taught you the architecture
of strength, form and glitz?

Your cradled nest
with its stolen haul of baubles high up on the mango tree.

If You Want the Flame to Dance Forever

This is not what you think it is:
a superb wine
in a crystal glass.
It's a fire
the kind that poets often conjure
from myths of dream, blood and bone.

Touch nothing,
and the flame will dance for ever
in its shimmering cage;
try diminishing it
and you'll have prose,
a wine close to vinegar;

feed it, and the fugitive fire
will take off with dodo wings,
turn strident the sweet line,
make hoarse the honey throat
as crystal shards bleed
on the polished floor.

Poem in the Light of Total Darkness

Listen: the poem has taken over.
With ears now exaggerated,
electric possibilities of sound,
every word falls clear
like rain on a tin roof.

Null and void are my drooping eyes,
flamboyant hair, my gravel voice.
Only the poem speaks
with the sea's haunting boom,
the delicate twitter of paddy birds.
Soon, the taste of honey and curd
will grow in your mouth.

Where sunlight,
or reading under fluorescence,
fashions the succubi of the mind,
blunts rhythms,
evening offers cherubim harps,
darkness with the sweet contradictions of stars.

And you will also see the firefly
with its belly-winking light,
lovers braid their limbs
with sweet syllables of fire,
night drawing silhouettes
of a loafing moon.

Or take the mango tree under sun-fire,

and you have description,
mere colour of fruit, green leaves.
By night, the magic shapes, smells
that suggest a season's glory, the spirit
lurking in the pith's dark juice.

As for my absence,
the voluntary stones in my mouth,
I know the prison of sunlight,
so I let the night
that holds the green poem
like a woman in its arms,
speak with love, with pure eloquence.

Roots

For Cleta Nora Marcellina Serpanchy

What the end usually demands
is something of the beginning,
and so
I conjure history from a cup
of warm Portuguese blood
from my forefathers
black diamond eyes, charcoal hair
from my Sinhalese mothers;
the beached catamaran,
gravel voices of the fishermen,
the catch still beating like a heart
under the pelting sun;
how the pariah dogs looked urgent
with fish-meal in their brains,
the children romped, sagged,
then melted into the sand.

A Portuguese captain holds
the soft brown hand of my Sinhala mother.
It's the year 1515 AD,
when two civilizations kissed and merged,
and I, burgher of that hot embrace,
write a poem of history
as if it were only the romance
of a lonely soldier on a crowded beach
in Southern Ceylon.

The Interview

Two TV cameras trained like guns,
I, the Sun-Man,
your caressing eyes,
and the countdown.

You coax me into beginnings,
past inventions in the snow,
then deftly persuade deeper fires,
my thin Canadian ice
to thaw in my throat,
the maple leaf smudge in my passport.

I am in the mouth of the sun,
the Immigrant's Song.
How I hear the elephant in my sleep,
white landscape in ruins.
I find my own, green forest, island sea,
the ocelot's eye, the jambu blood,
my childhood dream
in the claws of the sand crab.

And "what shaped your book
Flesh and Thorn?"
Blood on the sun,
the scarlet ibis blurred in the swamp,
how deceit crouched in the crotch,
"love, with his gift of pain."

Suddenly, I split the act in two,

juggle two red balls,
the poem made, the poem becoming.
I swim in your saucer eyes,
fingers search the curved fruit
under your shirt,
I nose ebony configurations,
dream the almond under the husk . . .

The Opposite Men

Once, sleep came easily
(without Sominex or Sleepeze)

Darkness fermented our dreams, traced
the brilliant vein of stars.

The bat excelled in its blind journeys,
we kept to paths of light.

Now we ransack night's silent bowl
with torch and headlamp, the pencil light of thieves,

Disco drums, beer bellies,
engines coughing along our highways.

From night we make the raw hunk of a Vegas day,
from day we learn to sleep in the hairy arms of the sloth.

We who are fat hunger to be thin,
the thin gorge themselves for bulk and curve.

We who are proud as stallions
seek loincloth and ashes for a single faddish day

And we who have bread
demand angel cake.

We are the opposite men,
found West when we should be East, North when South,

like Adam, caught again,
with the contrary apple in our mouth.

Poem for the Faltering Man

I'm balancing
on the brink

death and panorama
around and below.

But faltering legs
dangerous landscape

or final decisions
will not make the poem.

Only the supreme electricity
of doubt,

those screaming moments
when wind, muscle and mind

argue
whether to keep me up there

alive.

The Creative Process

He chooses
odd places
to write
his poems

like squatting
in a field
beside
an old cow
happily chewing
his cud

as it turns
out the poem
has nothing
to do
with the cow

except that it smells
of cow, cow breath
and cow dung.

Going for Broke

Michael O,
I tried your "trick with a knife"

but cut myself badly,
almost bled to death.
Which proves
that you cannot trust
the people you talk to, admire,
laugh with, read or read about.

How dangerous it is to try
those honoured prescriptions,
without first testing
one's own allergies,

and in the case of poetry
my own penchant
for the profound lie,
the bloodied flotsam
of immigrant men,
the batik and the exotic.

A Contrary Silence

How you wear a devil-dancer's mask
and move to the fevered drums;
then again, too often, too often,
I hear the cracking castanets,
the flamenco rhythm   drowning
the true song   the hush of soul
with the barefooted gypsy girl
dancing fire
in her swirl of skirt
as if all were right
with our bruising world.

"Know your own bone"—Thoreau

Is my heart's passionate dance
    but a moth flirting with the flame?
The long search   sweet discovery,
    you in dream,
the way you walked, walking
    with a Temple flower in your hair,
choosing denial, the Belladonna way.

What do I see, or choose to see
    by morning light?
Why does the mind always make choices
    for the eye?
You at the breakfast table,
    dispensing rituals
of Crispix cereal, orange juice, hot milk and toast;
    I, jousting with clock and laces,
winter boots that seem to shy
    from new journeys into the snow.

Night unravels the knotted muscle,
    makes room for dream, memory
that questions sad exits,
    chases the "whole bloody bird"
and ends up with a feather;
    must I remember the love I couldn't have,
forget the love of those I have?

Why, I ask my bones, is it harder to live
    than to die?

Death in minute doses, small martyrdoms,
    like noon's bland tuna sandwich,
the mailman's choice of junk mail and Christmas bills,
    road-salt and arthritis on my snow-shovelling hands,
the body's slow disarmament.

And when I unearth these bones again,
    gnaw at them slowly,
my father riding the mathematical surf
    like some Hawaiian beach boy,
as mother nurtures her restless brood of eight
    with curried and embracing love,
rattan cane;
    I see my wintered children
greening with summer,
    my grandson, Jens, throbbing and thriving
in his Viking snows

Dear Muse,
    this bone that lets me suck
the sweet marrow of words,
    is mine, stays here, is now—
no damp earth of burial,
    no unearthing shovel's bruise;
but why those first gestures
    of distrust?
how like a cruel sibling
    you once held the candy under my nose,
then snatched it away and laughed.

Now that you've
    offered me

the heart of the flute,
    be happy for the tapestries of my song,
the raven flies the world;
      I hear the immigrant's voice, sweet and clear
    as bamboo reed,
the elephant's trumpet
    shattering the dark silences
of the snow lands.

Death of a Poet

I got the word to sing
and the oriole sang,
the mynah bird called,
crow cleared its guttural throat.
You heard nothing.

I got the word to cry,
cry like the peacock
on the darkening brink of rain.
No blood drained your face,
no cry escaped your teeth.

I used the word like a scalpel
to probe the yellow wound.
You smelled no puss,
no adamant pain,
no crack in the crying skin.

I used the word softly
like a baby's milky gurgle,
But you held your head stiff,
glued your lips
to your own dark meanings.

I got the word to genuflect,
recite a holy rosary.
You saw no tabernacles,
sensed no gods, no saints,
just stared with those faithless eyes.

And so, you who never listened
to my green song,
behold the dream:
me, strangled by my own words
under a brown comforter,
the paramedics carrying
the mangled poem of my body,

and you sitting up
and listening at last.

Remains of an Asian Poet Writing in Canada

About the butterfly
that flapped
amber
in the cerebral land.

How winter
was made equal
to summer
and the skin glowed
like an oiled Brahmin
and bangles grew
on naked trees.

And summer
blew orioles
salad of mango
and the Bird of Paradise
draped its wings
on the concrete land.

They found
saffron wings
raw on a smooth stone.

The skull
separate   still green
in the dark wound
of a tree.

A thigh
bronze   warm
with the maul
of thorns.

And they found
the sun   dead
under the snow.

Elegy for the Unfinished Poem

Wildly started,
a single shot in the dark,
words splattered, mad
like birds in the din of bullets.
What remains is the ruined architecture
of stem and leaf, flotsam of feathers,
the falling heartbeat of a falling bird.

Nothing here sings.
The poet knows the colour of death,
the silence of the fallen.
The four geckos on the wall
look down with beady eyes,
their translucent bellies heavy
with the dead bones
of the once-dancing moths.
They listen for a poem,
then crawl away as the poet
embraces his still-born song,
the supreme blankness of his page,
the cruelty in the thought
that refuses to soar
above the darkening blur of words.

Poetry Reading at Scarborough College

Classroom H402,
way down Scarborough's concrete catacombs;
a hall of learning that suggests
some soulless architect,
a piece of civilization trapped like an animal.
and I am here, Pablo Neruda,
with only my fire and my song.

Fluorescent lamps bravely fake the sun,
pick up faces: young, sceptical, irreverent;
the host professor leans heavily on his cane
as he introduces the "SUN-MAN" poet.

Not a muscle moves. An audience, cold as concrete,
is up against my face.
What would you have done Pablo
in this landscape of ice?
Would you have insisted
that you were only "a man of bread and fish?"
That you would "not be found among books,
but with women and men
who have taught you the infinite"?

Yes. I'll fall back on myself,
ply these rapids with my bamboo oars.
So I give out my secrets
word by exotic word,
sing the truth to a *rabana* beat,
argue my metaphors of sun,

how the raven can match the eagle in flight,
the elephant dance on a pinhead!

And eyes question,
squint at sun meanings, laugh,
touch darkness, catch fire.
The Sun-Man poet reclaims the sun
as applause falls around him
like monsoon rain.

Requiem for the Passionate Ones

Think of those
who mourning their broken poems,
finally took the old poet's advice,
went quietly into the washroom
and slit their throats.

Think kindly,
for this was no cowardice or pablum,
but passion, passion,
the warm blood bubbling
in the final poem.

Think of those
who jumped the Golden Gate Bridge,
stained a summer sky
with their faithless arms,
limbs hopeless in the air,
an architecture
made crooked with despair.

Think kindly,
for they believed the karma
of hurtling arms,
the waters,
nibbhana at the end
of a passionate leap.

Think of those
who buried their heads

in the colourless flame—
how their lungs burst
the blue balloon of their pain,
leaving nothing
but a glaring light
in a sheaf of poems.

Think kindly,
of those who thought the road
never forked,
made absolute the end
before the beginning;
whose lives refused the darkness,
the incessant stoning;
who read death as a synonym for life,
and for one brief moment forgot
the colour of light.

And what are the ways
of passionate lovers?
I hear weeping
in old Verona, in the noble Houses
of Montague and Capulet.

"Dark with excessive bright"

Poet,
if these are poems
plucked from the mouth
of the sun,

why then
the crooked shadows,
night at high noon,
mahogany
pale with scars?

Do you have to spin
dark yarns
of silver fish grinning
with wood rot
in their mouths?

Why not fireflies
jewelling night,
or two-year-olds
bouncing the sun

in their sandbox,
or grass warm
as the blood of stars?

Dark I am,
and darkly do I sing
with mucus
in my throat,

for as soon
as I was born
under a banyan tree,
I heard prophecies,
a dying man cry:

O poet,
pitch your suns
where ghetto walls
foreclose the light,

be scalpel
cutting tumours
in your brother's brain,

be fire
for dried autumn leaves,
an archangel's trumpet
calling the dead to life.

I am
a dying voice
shaping words
for a wilderness,
for men crouched
with snow on their eyes,
ears dull as lead.

They will not, cannot
hear another song,
or read maps
to my island
in the sun   about

the Bird of Paradise
preening its feathers
in my brain,
green trees
fruiting in silence,
butterfly with laughing wings
still
under a dome.

Legacy

For Anne

"This is all there is and this is everything"—JOYCE CAROL OATES

Take my poems—
I have nothing else of value to give you.
fruits
of lonely nights, faithful candles
that flamed and sputtered until
my metaphors were right.

Take my poems—
my kingdom of fears in harness,
days of silence
when my neighbouring world
danced its tumultuous jig
and laughed.

Take my poems—
they were born with a brown skin,
sang with a brown voice,
danced a brown jig, persevered,
until the cold white paper
took in my words with the music
and fatted calf of the prodigal story.

Take my poems—
my umber heart my umber words,
the forgotten pain, the remembered music,
the new landscape,

why I thought God was a poem,
the poem, the only cosmic poet.

Take my poems—
mostly, because I love you,
they are the bloodstones
of my youth, fading footsteps of age,
small bouquets
that may, perhaps, survive a little while
like a memory.

Nothing else comes to mind—
the house is only wood and cabook,
the money is paper.

Acknowledgements

Some of these poems first appeared in the following journals: *Journal of South Asian Literature, Dalhousie Review, Ariel, Waves, UW Gazette, Confrontation, Toronto South Asian Review, Kunapipi, Imprint, Toronto Review of Contemporary Writing Abroad.*

PRAISE FOR RIENZI CRUSZ

"Arguably the best living Sri Lankan poet in English, though he has been in Canada since 1965, Crusz belongs to that older post-colonial generation, including such writers as Walcott and Soyinka, prepared to appropriate the colonial legacy of Shakespeare and English without anguished breast beating, 'as a tongue to speak with.'" —*World Literature Today*

"[Crusz] has much in common with such poets as W.B. Yeats, Dylan Thomas, Theodore Roethke and Irving Layton, embracing both the profane and the spiritual, the sexual and the sacred. Like William Blake, he recognizes that Everything that lives is Holy." —*The Record*

"At 84, the Waterloo poet knows a thing or two about mortality. His thoughts, musings and speculations, not to mention certainties and anxieties, are given eloquent expression in this deep, rich, moving meditative collection of poems that celebrate life as it reflects on death." —Robert Reid, *The Record*

"If you want to share a sensibility which is at once primitive and sophisticated, both intense and subtle, a poetic craft which is taut and concentrated, then read *Flesh and Thorn*." —*Quarry*

"Can Lit . . . has never articulated and transcended the experience of the incomer so wonderfully . . . the voice rings with a timbre known at once and altogether distinct; its range is abnormally large; its tone of infinite variety." —*The New Quarterly*

"I can't think of a single Canadian poet who, groin-tickled and happy, could achieve such delirium on paper. The raw passion is there despite the control the poems insist on. "

—Irving Layton

"His 'Immigrant's Song' is not only an attempt to come to terms with his own past, it is also a heroic statement of poetic independence." —Arun Mukherjee, *Currents*

"The cultural gift Crusz offers us, as a kind of magnificent verbal embroidery of the plain cloth of Canadian speech, continually surprises, delights, mystifies and liberates those of us raised on the sound of what Northrop Fry has called 'the Canadian goose honk.'"
—*The Toronto South Asian Review*

"Crusz, the most delicately nuanced (of such voices) uses his to balance a history, a role, and a difficult displacement . . . Like the West Indian poet, Derek Walcott [he] will not indulge in simplified opposition, whether of language, culture or colour."

—*Ariel*

"The Sun-Man poems are major artifacts of a new Canadian sensibility, important for the realities of our national selfhood."
—Nancy Lou Patterson, University of Waterloo

"Here was a true poetry of the displaced self, with sorrow beneath its bemused surface. Opposites—elephant and ice—are reconciled by a delightful wit, and ferocious though may be his interior heat, the light that the Sun-Man sheds upon the world lingers in the mind with a lovely after-glow."

—Zulfikar Ghose, University of Texas

"A most articulate poetry, with a fascinating sense of where you come from and where to."   —Robert Creely

"To call Crusz an immigrant poet is to summarize his intents too glibly. In both his books it is not the obvious contrast between elephant and ice, Sri Lanka and Canada, that is central but rather the manifold and specific ways in which a certain sensibility tries to cope honestly with perennial themes in both cultures."
                                                                    —Reshard Gool

"Crusz's language is subtle and he makes his points obliquely. Moreover, his self-examination always includes the social context of an immigrant's struggle for a sense of identity."
                                                                    —*Books in Canada*

"His real genius lies not in the message contained in the poetry, but in the pursuit of perfection in poetic form. Very much a poet of sound and rhythm, Crusz writes with an awareness that poetry is about language, about the power of imagination. He is a very self –conscious poet, and that is precisely why his reputation will outlast that of his contemporaries."
                                        —Chelva Kanaganayakam, University of Toronto